This book belongs to:

_____

_____

_____

# Friends

An address book for those who
cherish the joys of friendship

⁓

Illustrated by
## Donna Green

SMITHMARK

This edition published in 1995 by SMITHMARK Publishers Inc.
16 East 32nd Street, New York, NY 10016

SMITHMARK books are available for bulk purchase for
sales promotions and premium use.
For details write or telephone the manager of special sales,
SMITHMARK Publishers, Inc., 16 East 32nd Street
New York, NY 10016; (212) 532-6600

Produced by VIA Rob Fremont, Inc.
c/o Vermilion
P.O. Box 144
Norwell, MA 02061

*A Rob Fremont Book*

Design by Berge Zerdelian
Editor: Oliver Fremont
Composition: Garbo Typesetting

ISBN: 0-8317-3198-2

Printed and bound in China by Imago Publishing Ltd

10 9 8 7 6 5 4 3 2 1

# List of Paintings

A . . . . . . . . . . . . . *Jessica's Tea Party*
*Baking Gingerbread*

B . . . . . . . . . . . . . *Christmas Eve*

C . . . . . . . . . . . . . *The Fir Tree*
*Christina's Secret Garden*

D . . . . . . . . . . . . . *A Moment in Time*

E . . . . . . . . . . . . . *Picking Blueberries*

F . . . . . . . . . . . . . *Block City*

G . . . . . . . . . . . . . *Alissa's Flock*

H . . . . . . . . . . . . . *Story Time*

IJ . . . . . . . . . . . . . *Amanda & Monique*

K . . . . . . . . . . . . . *Sugar n' Spice*

L . . . . . . . . . . . . . *Puppy Love*

M . . . . . . . . . . . . . *Once Upon A Time*

N . . . . . . . . . . . . . *Sand Castle*

O . . . . . . . . . . . . . *I Can Do It Myself*

P . . . . . . . . . . . . . *Feeding the Ducks*

QR . . . . . . . . . . . . *A Few of My Favorite Things*

S . . . . . . . . . . . . . *Let's Pretend*

T . . . . . . . . . . . . . *A Fairy Tale Day*

UV . . . . . . . . . . . *At Grandma's Knee*

W . . . . . . . . . . . . . *Elizabeth's Afternoon Tea*

NOTES . . . . . . . . *Toasty Inside*
*Four Little Ballerinas*

*W*hoever is happy will make others happy too.

– ANNE FRANK

Name                                    Telephone

Address

_____             _____

_____             _____

_____             _____


Name                                    Telephone

Address

_____             _____

_____             _____

_____             _____


Name                                    Telephone

Address

_____             _____

_____             _____

_____             _____


Name                                    Telephone

Address

_____             _____

_____             _____

_____             _____

*A*

Name _____     Telephone _____

Address _____     _____

_____     _____

_____     _____

Name _____     Telephone _____

Address _____     _____

_____     _____

_____     _____

Name _____     Telephone _____

Address _____     _____

_____     _____

_____     _____

Name _____     Telephone _____

Address _____     _____

_____     _____

_____     _____

**F**riendship with oneself is all important, because without it one cannot be
friends with anyone else in the world.     – ELEANOR ROOSEVELT

A

Name _____  Telephone _____

Address _____  _____

_____  _____

_____  _____


Name _____  Telephone _____

Address _____  _____

_____  _____

_____  _____


Name _____  Telephone _____

Address _____  _____

_____  _____

_____  _____


Name _____  Telephone _____

Address _____  _____

_____  _____

_____  _____

*A*

*Name* _____   *Telephone* _____

*Address* _____   _____

_____   _____

_____   _____

*Name* _____   *Telephone* _____

*Address* _____   _____

_____   _____

_____   _____

*Name* _____   *Telephone* _____

*Address* _____   _____

_____   _____

_____   _____

*Name* _____   *Telephone* _____

*Address* _____   _____

_____   _____

_____   _____

*Name* _____   *Telephone* _____

*Address* _____   _____

_____   _____

_____   _____

*A* friend is a present you give yourself.
– ROBERT LOUIS STEVENSON

A

Name _____ Telephone _____

Address _____ _____

_____ _____

_____ _____

Name _____ Telephone _____

Address _____

_____ _____

_____ _____

Name _____ Telephone _____

Address _____ _____

_____ _____

_____ _____

Name _____ Telephone _____

Address _____ _____

_____ _____

_____ _____

Name _____ Telephone _____

Address _____ _____

_____ _____

_____ _____

Name _____    Telephone _____

Address _____    _____

_____    _____

_____    _____


Name _____    Telephone _____

Address _____    _____

_____    _____

_____    _____


Name _____    Telephone _____

Address _____    _____

_____    _____

_____    _____


Name _____    Telephone _____

Address _____    _____

_____    _____

_____    _____

"Stay" is a charming word in a friend's vocabulary.
–LOUISA MAY ALCOTT

*B*

Name

Telephone

Address

Name

Telephone

Address

Name

Telephone

Address

Name

Telephone

Address

Name _____  Telephone _____

Address _____

_____  _____

_____  _____

_____  _____


Name _____  Telephone _____

Address _____

_____  _____

_____  _____

_____  _____


Name _____  Telephone _____

Address _____

_____  _____

_____  _____

_____  _____


Name _____  Telephone _____

Address _____

_____  _____

_____  _____

_____  _____


*As you say, we don't need soft skies to make friendship a joy to us. What a heavenly thing it is; "World without end," truly. I grow warm thinking of it, and should glow at the thought if all the glaciers of the Alps were heaped over me!* —CELIA THAXTER

*Name* _____  *Telephone* _____

*Address* _____ _____

_____ _____

_____ _____

_____ _____

*Name* _____  *Telephone* _____

*Address* _____ _____

_____ _____

_____ _____

_____ _____

*Name* _____  *Telephone* _____

*Address* _____ _____

_____ _____

_____ _____

_____ _____

*Name* _____  *Telephone* _____

*Address* _____ _____

_____ _____

_____ _____

_____ _____

Name _____    Telephone _____

Address _____    _____

_____    _____

_____    _____


Name _____    Telephone _____

Address _____    _____

_____    _____

_____    _____


Name _____    Telephone _____

Address _____    _____

_____    _____

_____    _____


Name _____    Telephone _____

Address _____    _____

_____    _____

_____    _____


*Make happy those who are near, and those who are far will come.*
– CHINESE PROVERB

*B*

*Name* _____  *Telephone* _____

*Address* _____  _____

_____  _____

_____  _____

*Name* _____  *Telephone* _____

*Address* _____  _____

_____  _____

_____  _____

*Name* _____  *Telephone* _____

*Address* _____  _____

_____  _____

_____  _____

*Name* _____  *Telephone* _____

*Address* _____  _____

_____  _____

_____  _____

*Name* _____  *Telephone* _____

*Address* _____  _____

_____  _____

_____  _____

*O*nce the children were in the house the air became more vivid and more heated; every object in the house grew more alive.

– MARY GORDON

*B*

Name _____     Telephone _____

Address _____     _____
_____     _____
_____     _____

Name _____     Telephone _____

Address _____     _____
_____     _____
_____     _____

Name _____     Telephone _____

Address _____     _____
_____     _____
_____     _____

Name _____     Telephone _____

Address _____     _____
_____     _____
_____     _____

*If we would build on a sure foundation in friendship, we must
love our friends for their sakes rather than for our own.*

–CHARLOTTE BRONTË

*B*

| *Name* | *Telephone* |
|---|---|
| *Address* | |

| *Name* | *Telephone* |
|---|---|
| *Address* | |

| *Name* | *Telephone* |
|---|---|
| *Address* | |

| *Name* | *Telephone* |
|---|---|
| *Address* | |

| *Name* | *Telephone* |
|---|---|
| *Address* | |

*C*

Name _____ Telephone _____

Address _____ _____

_____ _____

_____ _____


Name _____ Telephone _____

Address _____ _____

_____ _____

_____ _____


Name _____ Telephone _____

Address _____ _____

_____ _____

_____ _____


Name _____ Telephone _____

Address _____ _____

_____ _____

_____ _____

Name _____ Telephone _____

Address _____ _____

_____ _____

_____ _____

Name _____ Telephone _____

Address _____ _____

_____ _____

_____ _____

Name _____ Telephone _____

Address _____ _____

_____ _____

_____ _____

Name _____ Telephone _____

Address _____ _____

_____ _____

_____ _____

**H**appiness is not a state to arrive at, but a manner of traveling.
– MARGARET LEE RUNBECK

*C*

*Name* _____  *Telephone* _____

*Address* _____  _____

_____  _____

_____  _____


*Name* _____  *Telephone* _____

*Address* _____  _____

_____  _____

_____  _____


*Name* _____  *Telephone* _____

*Address* _____  _____

_____  _____

_____  _____


*Name* _____  *Telephone* _____

*Address* _____  _____

_____  _____

_____  _____


*Name* _____  *Telephone* _____

*Address* _____  _____

_____  _____

_____  _____

*On the road between the homes of friends, grass does not grow.*

– NORWEGIAN PROVERB

*C*

Name _____     Telephone _____

Address _____     _____

_____     _____

_____     _____


Name _____     Telephone _____

Address _____     _____

_____     _____

_____     _____


Name _____     Telephone _____

Address _____     _____

_____     _____

_____     _____


Name _____     Telephone _____

Address _____     _____

_____     _____

_____     _____


Name _____     Telephone _____

Address _____     _____

_____     _____

_____     _____

Name _____  Telephone _____

Address _____

_____

_____

Name _____  Telephone _____

Address _____

_____

_____

Name _____  Telephone _____

Address _____

_____

_____

Name _____  Telephone _____

Address _____

_____

_____

_____

You can lay the foundation of friendship in a matter of moments, but it is a work of time to build a monument.

—MADELYN WATT

*C*

Name _____  Telephone _____

Address _____  _____

_____  _____

_____  _____

Name _____  Telephone _____

Address _____  _____

_____  _____

_____  _____

Name _____  Telephone _____

Address _____  _____

_____  _____

_____  _____

Name _____  Telephone _____

Address _____  _____

_____  _____

_____  _____

Name _____  Telephone _____

Address _____  _____

_____  _____

_____  _____

*The only rose without thorns is friendship.*
– MADELEINE de SCUDERY

D

*D*

| Name | Telephone |
|------|-----------|
| Address | |

| Name | Telephone |
|------|-----------|
| Address | |

| Name | Telephone |
|------|-----------|
| Address | |

| Name | Telephone |
|------|-----------|
| Address | |

*Name*

*Telephone*

*Address*

*Name*

*Telephone*

*Address*

*Name*

*Telephone*

*Address*

*Name*

*Telephone*

*Address*

N*ow may the warming love of friends*
*Surround you as you go*
*Down the path of light and laughter*
*Where the happy memories grow.*
–HELEN LOWRIE MARSHALL

D

| Name | Telephone |
|------|-----------|
| Address | |
| | |
| | |

| Name | Telephone |
|------|-----------|
| Address | |
| | |
| | |

| Name | Telephone |
|------|-----------|
| Address | |
| | |
| | |

| Name | Telephone |
|------|-----------|
| Address | |
| | |
| | |

Name _____    Telephone _____

Address _____    _____

_____    _____

_____    _____


Name _____    Telephone _____

Address _____    _____

_____    _____

_____    _____


Name _____    Telephone _____

Address _____    _____

_____    _____

_____    _____


Name _____    Telephone _____

Address _____    _____

_____    _____

_____    _____


*Wear a smile and have friends; Wear a scowl and have wrinkles. What do we live for if not to make the world less difficult for each other?*

– GEORGE ELIOT

D

Name _____ Telephone _____

Address _____ _____

_____ _____

_____ _____

Name _____ Telephone _____

Address _____ _____

_____ _____

_____ _____

Name _____ Telephone _____

Address _____ _____

_____ _____

_____ _____

Name _____ Telephone _____

Address _____ _____

_____ _____

_____ _____

Name _____ Telephone _____

Address _____ _____

_____ _____

_____ _____

*M*ake-believe colors the past with innocent distortion, and it swirls ahead of us in a thousand ways . . . It is part of our collective lives, entwining our past and our future.

– SHIRLEY TEMPLE BLACK

*D*

Name _____ Telephone _____

Address _____ _____

_____ _____

_____ _____

Name _____ Telephone _____

Address _____ _____

_____ _____

_____ _____

Name _____ Telephone _____

Address _____ _____

_____ _____

_____ _____

Name _____ Telephone _____

Address _____ _____

_____ _____

_____ _____

Name _____ Telephone _____

Address _____ _____

_____ _____

_____ _____

Name _____  Telephone _____

Address _____  _____

_____  _____

_____  _____

Name _____  Telephone _____

Address _____  _____

_____  _____

_____  _____

Name _____  Telephone _____

Address _____  _____

_____  _____

_____  _____

Name _____  Telephone _____

Address _____  _____

_____  _____

_____  _____

*I always felt that the great high privilege, relief and comfort of friendship was that one had to explain nothing.*

– KATHERINE MANSFIELD

*E*

Name

Telephone

Address

Name

Telephone

Address

Name

Telephone

Address

Name

Telephone

Address

Name _____    Telephone _____

Address _____    _____

_____    _____

_____    _____


Name _____    Telephone _____

Address _____    _____

_____    _____

_____    _____


Name _____    Telephone _____

Address _____    _____

_____    _____

_____    _____


Name _____    Telephone _____

Address _____    _____

_____    _____

_____    _____


*S*hared joy is double joy, and shared sorrow is half-sorrow.
– SWEDISH PROVERB

*A*nd the song from beginning to end, I found in the heart of a friend.

– HENRY WADSWORTH LONGFELLOW

*E*

Name _____  Telephone _____

Address _____ _____

_____ _____

_____ _____

Name _____  Telephone _____

Address _____ _____

_____ _____

_____ _____

Name _____  Telephone _____

Address _____ _____

_____ _____

_____ _____

Name _____  Telephone _____

Address _____ _____

_____ _____

_____ _____

Name _____  Telephone _____

Address _____ _____

_____ _____

_____ _____

F

*F*

| | |
|---|---|
| *Name* | *Telephone* |
| *Address* | |

| | |
|---|---|
| *Name* | *Telephone* |
| *Address* | |

| | |
|---|---|
| *Name* | *Telephone* |
| *Address* | |

| | |
|---|---|
| *Name* | *Telephone* |
| *Address* | |

F

Name                                          Telephone

Address


Name                                          Telephone

Address


Name                                          Telephone

Address


Name                                          Telephone

Address


*There was nothing remote or mysterious here – only something private.
The only secret was the ancient communication between two people.*

— EUDORA WELTY

*Is nothing in life ever straight and clear; the way children see it.*

–ROSIE THOMAS

Name

Telephone

Address

---

Name

Telephone

Address

---

Name

Telephone

Address

---

Name

Telephone

Address

---

Name

Telephone

Address

*F*

*Name*                                    *Telephone*

*Address*

---

*Name*                                    *Telephone*

*Address*

---

*Name*                                    *Telephone*

*Address*

---

*Name*                                    *Telephone*

*Address*

---

*Name*                                    *Telephone*

*Address*

Name _____  Telephone _____

Address _____  _____

_____  _____

_____  _____


Name _____  Telephone _____

Address _____  _____

_____  _____

_____  _____


Name _____  Telephone _____

Address _____  _____

_____  _____

_____  _____


Name _____  Telephone _____

Address _____  _____

_____  _____

_____  _____


Name _____  Telephone _____

Address _____  _____

_____  _____

_____  _____

G

*G*

| Name | Telephone |
|------|-----------|
| Address | |

| Name | Telephone |
|------|-----------|
| Address | |

| Name | Telephone |
|------|-----------|
| Address | |

| Name | Telephone |
|------|-----------|
| Address | |

Name _____  Telephone _____

Address _____  _____

_____  _____

_____  _____

Name _____  Telephone _____

Address _____  _____

_____  _____

_____  _____

Name _____  Telephone _____

Address _____  _____

_____  _____

_____  _____

Name _____  Telephone _____

Address _____  _____

_____  _____

_____  _____

*My friends are my estate. Forgive me then the avarice to hoard them. They tell me those who were poor early have different views of gold. I don't know how that is. God is not so wary as we, else He would give us no friends lest we forget him.* —EMILY DICKINSON

*If a child lives with criticism,*
*He learns to condemn.*
*If a child lives with hostility,*
*He learns to fight.*
*If a child lives with ridicule,*
*He learns to be shy.*
*If a child lives with shame,*
*He learns to feel guilty.*
*If a child lives with tolerance,*
*He learns to be patient.*
*If a child lives with encouragement,*
*He learns confidence.*
*If a child lives with fairness,*
*He learns justice.*
*If a child lives with security,*
*He learns to like himself.*
*If a child lives with acceptance and friendship,*
*He learns to find love in the world.*

–DOROTHY L. NOLTE

G

Name _____  Telephone _____

Address _____  _____

_____  _____

_____  _____


Name _____  Telephone _____

Address _____  _____

_____  _____

_____  _____


Name _____  Telephone _____

Address _____  _____

_____  _____

_____  _____


Name _____  Telephone _____

Address _____  _____

_____  _____

_____  _____


Name _____  Telephone _____

Address _____  _____

_____  _____

*H*

Name _____  Telephone _____

Address _____  _____

_____  _____

_____  _____

Name _____  Telephone _____

Address _____  _____

_____  _____

_____  _____

Name _____  Telephone _____

Address _____  _____

_____  _____

_____  _____

Name _____  Telephone _____

Address _____  _____

_____  _____

_____  _____

Name _____  Telephone _____

Address _____  _____

_____  _____

_____  _____


Name _____  Telephone _____

Address _____  _____

_____  _____

_____  _____


Name _____  Telephone _____

Address _____  _____

_____  _____

_____  _____


Name _____  Telephone _____

Address _____  _____

_____  _____

_____  _____


*What the heart gives away is never gone . . . It is kept in the hearts of others.*

—ROBIN ST. JOHN

*There is no frigate like a book to take us lands away*
*Nor any courses like a page of prancing poetry*
*This traverse may the poorest take without oppress of toil*
*How frugal is the chariot that bears the human soul!*

– EMILY DICKINSON

H

Name _____     Telephone _____

Address _____     _____

_____     _____

_____     _____

Name _____     Telephone _____

Address _____     _____

_____     _____

_____     _____

Name _____     Telephone _____

Address _____     _____

_____     _____

_____     _____

Name _____     Telephone _____

Address _____     _____

_____     _____

_____     _____

Name _____     Telephone _____

Address _____     _____

_____     _____

_____     _____

*I J*

| | |
|---|---|
| Name | Telephone |
| Address | |
| | |
| | |
| | |

| | |
|---|---|
| Name | Telephone |
| Address | |
| | |
| | |
| | |

| | |
|---|---|
| Name | Telephone |
| Address | |
| | |
| | |
| | |

| | |
|---|---|
| Name | Telephone |
| Address | |
| | |
| | |
| | |

Name _____     Telephone _____

Address _____     _____

_____     _____

_____     _____

_____     _____


Name _____     Telephone _____

Address _____     _____

_____     _____

_____     _____

_____     _____


Name _____     Telephone _____

Address _____     _____

_____     _____

_____     _____

_____     _____


Name _____     Telephone _____

Address _____     _____

_____     _____

_____     _____

_____     _____


The healthy and strong individual is the one who asks for help when
he needs it, whether he's got an abscess on his knee or in his soul.

– RONA BARRET

*S*ilences make the real conversations between friends. Not the
saying but the never needing to say is what counts.

– MARGARET LEE RUNBECK

Name                                    Telephone

Address

Name                                    Telephone

Address

Name                                    Telephone

Address

Name                                    Telephone

Address

Name                                    Telephone

Address

*K*

Name _____     Telephone _____

Address _____     _____

_____     _____

_____     _____


Name _____     Telephone _____

Address _____     _____

_____     _____

_____     _____


Name _____     Telephone _____

Address _____     _____

_____     _____

_____     _____


Name _____     Telephone _____

Address _____     _____

_____     _____

_____     _____

K

Name _____    Telephone _____

Address _____    _____

_____    _____

_____    _____


Name _____    Telephone _____

Address _____    _____

_____    _____

_____    _____


Name _____    Telephone _____

Address _____    _____

_____    _____

_____    _____


Name _____    Telephone _____

Address _____    _____

_____    _____

_____    _____


*W*here you used to be, there is a hole in the world, which I find myself
constantly walking around in the daytime, and falling into at night.
I miss you like hell.          — EDNA ST. VINCENT MILLAY

*K*

*Name* _____  *Telephone* _____

*Address* _____  _____

_____  _____

_____  _____

*Name* _____  *Telephone* _____

*Address* _____  _____

_____  _____

_____  _____

*Name* _____  *Telephone* _____

*Address* _____  _____

_____  _____

_____  _____

*Name* _____  *Telephone* _____

*Address* _____  _____

_____  _____

_____  _____

*Name* _____  *Telephone* _____

*Address* _____  _____

_____  _____

_____  _____

*W*hat are little girls made of, made of?
What are little girls made of?
Sugar and spice, and all things nice,
That's what little girls are made of, made of.

– ANON

*L*

| | |
|---|---|
| Name | Telephone |
| Address | |
| | |
| | |
| | |

| | |
|---|---|
| Name | Telephone |
| Address | |
| | |
| | |
| | |

| | |
|---|---|
| Name | Telephone |
| Address | |
| | |
| | |
| | |

| | |
|---|---|
| Name | Telephone |
| Address | |
| | |
| | |
| | |

L

Name                                    Telephone

Address

_____

_____

Name                                    Telephone

Address

_____

_____

Name                                    Telephone

Address

_____

_____

Name                                    Telephone

Address

_____

_____

*Constant use had not worn ragged the fabric of their friendship.*
— DOROTHY PARKER

*L*

*Name* _____    *Telephone* _____

*Address* _____    _____

_____    _____

_____    _____

*Name* _____    *Telephone* _____

*Address* _____    _____

_____    _____

_____    _____

*Name* _____    *Telephone* _____

*Address* _____    _____

_____    _____

_____    _____

*Name* _____    *Telephone* _____

*Address* _____    _____

_____    _____

_____    _____

*Name* _____    *Telephone* _____

*Address* _____    _____

_____    _____

_____    _____

$W$hat are little boys made of, made of?
What are little boys made of?
Snips and snails, and puppy-dog's tails;
That's what little boys are made of, made of.

– ANON

*L*

*Name* _____    *Telephone* _____

*Address* _____    _____

_____    _____

_____    _____


*Name* _____    *Telephone* _____

*Address* _____    _____

_____    _____

_____    _____


*Name* _____    *Telephone* _____

*Address* _____    _____

_____    _____

_____    _____


*Name* _____    *Telephone* _____

*Address* _____    _____

_____    _____

_____    _____

Name _____  Telephone _____

Address _____  _____

_____  _____

_____  _____

Name _____  Telephone _____

Address _____  _____

_____  _____

_____  _____

Name _____  Telephone _____

Address _____  _____

_____  _____

_____  _____

Name _____  Telephone _____

Address _____  _____

_____  _____

_____  _____

*One's life has value so long as one attributes value to the life of others, by means of love, friendship, indignation and compassion.*

— SIMONE DE BEAUVOIR

# M

*Name*

*Address*

*Telephone*

---

*Name*

*Address*

*Telephone*

---

*Name*

*Address*

*Telephone*

---

*Name*

*Address*

*Telephone*

Name _____  Telephone _____

Address _____  _____

_____  _____

_____  _____

Name _____  Telephone _____

Address _____  _____

_____  _____

_____  _____

Name _____  Telephone _____

Address _____  _____

_____  _____

_____  _____

Name _____  Telephone _____

Address _____  _____

_____  _____

_____  _____

**Y**es'm, old friends is always best, 'less you can catch a new one
that's fit to make an old one out of.

—SARAH ORNE JEWETT

*M*

Name _____     Telephone _____

Address _____     _____

_____     _____

_____     _____

_____     _____

Name _____     Telephone _____

Address _____     _____

_____     _____

_____     _____

Name _____     Telephone _____

Address _____     _____

_____     _____

_____     _____

Name _____     Telephone _____

Address _____     _____

_____     _____

_____     _____

*Some of the finest friendships are between persons of different dispositions. The mind is often attracted by perfections it lacks itself.*

– EUSTACE BUDGELL

*M*

Name _____          Telephone _____

Address _____       _____

_____               _____

_____               _____


Name _____          Telephone _____

Address _____       _____

_____               _____

_____               _____


Name _____          Telephone _____

Address _____       _____

_____               _____

_____               _____


Name _____          Telephone _____

Address _____       _____

_____               _____

_____               _____


Name _____          Telephone _____

Address _____       _____

_____               _____

_____               _____

*M*

Name _____  Telephone _____

Address _____
_____
_____

Name _____  Telephone _____

Address _____
_____
_____

Name _____  Telephone _____

Address _____
_____
_____

Name _____  Telephone _____

Address _____
_____
_____

Name _____  Telephone _____

Address _____
_____
_____

*E*ach friend represents a world in us, a world possibly not born
until they arrive, and it is only by this meeting that a new world
is born.
                                                              −ANAÏS NIN

*M*

Name _____          Telephone _____

Address _____                   _____

_____                   _____

_____                   _____

_____                   _____

Name _____          Telephone _____

Address _____                   _____

_____                   _____

_____                   _____

_____                   _____

Name _____          Telephone _____

Address _____                   _____

_____                   _____

_____                   _____

_____                   _____

Name _____          Telephone _____

Address _____                   _____

_____                   _____

_____                   _____

_____                   _____

Name _____          Telephone _____

Address _____                   _____

_____                   _____

_____                   _____

_____                   _____

Name _____     Telephone _____

Address _____     _____

_____     _____

_____     _____


Name _____     Telephone _____

Address _____     _____

_____     _____

_____     _____


Name _____     Telephone _____

Address _____     _____

_____     _____

_____     _____


Name _____     Telephone _____

Address _____     _____

_____     _____

_____     _____

*Hold a true friend with both your hands.*
—NIGERIAN PROVERB

*N*

| | |
|---|---|
| Name | Telephone |
| Address | |

| | |
|---|---|
| Name | Telephone |
| Address | |

| | |
|---|---|
| Name | Telephone |
| Address | |

| | |
|---|---|
| Name | Telephone |
| Address | |

Name _____    Telephone _____

Address _____    _____

_____    _____

_____    _____


Name _____    Telephone _____

Address _____    _____

_____    _____

_____    _____


Name _____    Telephone _____

Address _____    _____

_____    _____

_____    _____


Name _____    Telephone _____

Address _____    _____

_____    _____

_____    _____


The human heart, at whatever age, opens only
to the heart that opens in return.

– MARIE EDGEWORTH

N

Name _____ Telephone _____

Address _____ _____
_____ _____
_____ _____

Name _____ Telephone _____

Address _____ _____
_____ _____
_____ _____

Name _____ Telephone _____

Address _____ _____
_____ _____
_____ _____

Name _____ Telephone _____

Address _____ _____
_____ _____
_____ _____

Name _____ Telephone _____

Address _____ _____
_____ _____
_____ _____

*M*y only sketch, profile, of Heaven is a large blue sky, and larger than the biggest I have seen in June – and in it are my friends – every one of them.
                                                        –EMILY DICKINSON

*N*

Name _____  Telephone _____

Address _____  _____

_____  _____

_____  _____


Name _____  Telephone _____

Address _____  _____

_____  _____

_____  _____


Name _____  Telephone _____

Address _____  _____

_____  _____

_____  _____


Name _____  Telephone _____

Address _____  _____

_____  _____

_____  _____


Name _____  Telephone _____

Address _____  _____

_____  _____

_____  _____

Name

Telephone

Address

---

Name

Telephone

Address

---

Name

Telephone

Address

---

Two may talk together under the same roof for many years, yet never really meet; and two others at first speech are old friends.

– MARY CATHERWOOD

*O*

| | |
|---|---|
| Name | Telephone |
| Address | |

| | |
|---|---|
| Name | Telephone |
| Address | |

| | |
|---|---|
| Name | Telephone |
| Address | |

| | |
|---|---|
| Name | Telephone |
| Address | |

Name _____     Telephone _____

Address _____     _____

_____     _____

_____     _____


Name _____     Telephone _____

Address _____     _____

_____     _____

_____     _____


Name _____     Telephone _____

Address _____     _____

_____     _____

_____     _____


Name _____     Telephone _____

Address _____     _____

_____     _____

_____     _____


**A** *gentle word, like summer rain,*
*May soothe some heart and banish pain.*
*What joy or sadness often springs*
*From just the simple little things!*

— WILLA HOEY

. . . *W*hat *do girls do who haven't any mothers to help them through their troubles?*

–LOUISA MAY ALCOTT

Name _____     Telephone _____

Address _____     _____

_____     _____

_____     _____

_____     _____

Name _____     Telephone _____

Address _____     _____

_____     _____

_____     _____

_____     _____

Name _____     Telephone _____

Address _____     _____

_____     _____

_____     _____

_____     _____

Name _____     Telephone _____

Address _____     _____

_____     _____

_____     _____

_____     _____

Name _____     Telephone _____

Address _____     _____

_____     _____

_____     _____

*P*

Name

Telephone

Address

___

___

___

Name

Telephone

Address

___

___

___

Name

Telephone

Address

___

___

___

Name

Telephone

Address

___

___

___

Name _____    Telephone _____

Address _____    _____

_____    _____

_____    _____

Name _____    Telephone _____

Address _____    _____

_____    _____

_____    _____

Name _____    Telephone _____

Address _____    _____

_____    _____

_____    _____

Name _____    Telephone _____

Address _____    _____

_____    _____

_____    _____

*We cannot really love anybody with whom we never laugh.*
– A. REPPLIER

*P*

*Name*

*Telephone*

*Address*

*Name*

*Telephone*

*Address*

*Name*

*Telephone*

*Address*

*Name*

*Telephone*

*Address*

*Name*

*Telephone*

*Address*

. . . *W*hat do we live for if not to make the world less difficult for each other.

– GEORGE ELIOT

Name _____  Telephone _____

Address _____  _____

_____  _____

_____

_____

Name _____  Telephone _____

Address _____  _____

_____  _____

_____  _____

Name _____  Telephone _____

Address _____  _____

_____  _____

_____  _____

Name _____  Telephone _____

Address _____  _____

_____  _____

_____  _____

*The truth is friendship is every bit as sacred and eternal as marriage.*
— KATHERINE MANSFIELD

*P*

Name                                        Telephone

Address

_____

_____

Name                                        Telephone

Address

_____

_____

Name                                        Telephone

Address

_____

_____

Name                                        Telephone

Address

_____

_____

$\mathcal{Q} \ \mathcal{R}$

Name _____ Telephone _____

Address _____ _____

_____ _____

_____ _____

Name _____ Telephone _____

Address _____ _____

_____ _____

_____ _____

Name _____ Telephone _____

Address _____ _____

_____ _____

_____ _____

Name _____ Telephone _____

Address _____ _____

_____ _____

_____ _____

Q<sub>R</sub>

Name _____     Telephone _____

Address _____     _____

_____     _____

_____     _____


Name _____     Telephone _____

Address _____     _____

_____     _____

_____     _____


Name _____     Telephone _____

Address _____     _____

_____     _____

_____     _____


Name _____     Telephone _____

Address _____     _____

_____     _____

_____     _____

Treat your friends as you do your paintings,
and place them in the best light.
— JENNIE JEROME CHURCHILL

$Q^R$

Name _____    Telephone _____

Address _____    _____

_____    _____

_____    _____

Name _____    Telephone _____

Address _____    _____

_____    _____

_____    _____

Name _____    Telephone _____

Address _____    _____

_____    _____

_____    _____

Name _____    Telephone _____

Address _____    _____

_____    _____

_____    _____

Name _____    Telephone _____

Address _____    _____

_____    _____

_____    _____

*The little things
That make life sweet
Are worth their weight in gold;
They can't be bought
At any price
And neither are they sold.*

– ESTELLE WAITE HOOVER

$Q^R$

Name _____ Telephone _____

Address _____ _____

_____ _____

_____ _____

Name _____ Telephone _____

Address _____ _____

_____ _____

_____ _____

Name _____ Telephone _____

Address _____ _____

_____ _____

_____ _____

Name _____ Telephone _____

Address _____ _____

_____ _____

_____ _____

Name _____ Telephone _____

Address _____ _____

_____ _____

_____ _____

Name _____  Telephone _____

Address _____  _____

_____  _____

_____  _____

Name _____  Telephone _____

Address _____  _____

_____  _____

_____  _____

Name _____  Telephone _____

Address _____  _____

_____  _____

_____  _____

Name _____  Telephone _____

Address _____  _____

_____  _____

_____  _____

**I**f there is anything better than to be loved it is loving.

– ANON

Name _____    Telephone _____

Address _____    _____

_____    _____

_____    _____

_____    _____


Name _____    Telephone _____

Address _____    _____

_____    _____

_____    _____

_____    _____


Name _____    Telephone _____

Address _____    _____

_____    _____

_____    _____

_____    _____


Name _____    Telephone _____

Address _____    _____

_____    _____

_____    _____

_____    _____

Name _____    Telephone _____

Address _____    _____

_____    _____

_____    _____


Name _____    Telephone _____

Address _____    _____

_____    _____

_____    _____


Name _____    Telephone _____

Address _____    _____

_____    _____

_____    _____


Name _____    Telephone _____

Address _____    _____

_____    _____

_____    _____


*That is the best - to laugh with someone because
you both think the same things are funny.*

–GLORIA VANDERBILT

S

Name

Address

Telephone

Name

Address

Telephone

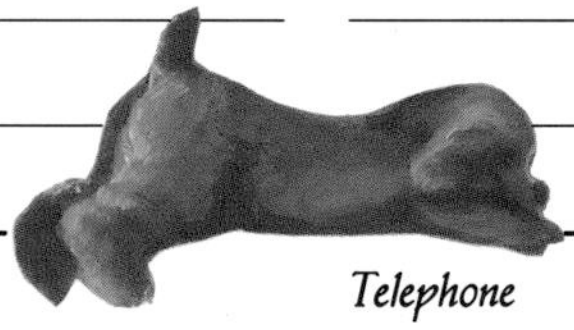

Name

Address

Telephone

Name

Address

Telephone

Name

Address

Telephone

S

Name _____     Telephone _____

Address _____                _____

_____                _____

_____                _____

Name _____     Telephone _____

Address _____                _____

_____                _____

_____                _____

Name _____     Telephone _____

Address _____                _____

_____                _____

_____                _____

Name _____     Telephone _____

Address _____                _____

_____                _____

_____                _____

Happiness is a sunbeam which may pass through a thousand bosoms
without losing a particle of its original ray; nay, when it strikes on a
kindred heart, like the converged light on a mirror, it reflects itself with
redoubled brightness. It is not perfected till it is shared.

– JANE PORTER

S

Name _____ Telephone _____

Address _____ _____

_____ _____

_____ _____

Name _____ Telephone _____

Address _____ _____

_____ _____

_____ _____

Name _____ Telephone _____

Address _____ _____

_____ _____

_____ _____

Name _____ Telephone _____

Address _____ _____

_____ _____

_____ _____

Name _____ Telephone _____

Address _____ _____

_____ _____

_____ _____

*T*he events of childhood do not pass but repeat themselves like seasons of the year.

– ELEANOR FARJEON

S

Name _____ Telephone _____

Address _____ _____

_____ _____

_____ _____

Name _____ Telephone _____

Address _____ _____

_____ _____

_____ _____

Name _____ Telephone _____

Address _____ _____

_____ _____

_____ _____

Name _____ Telephone _____

Address _____ _____

_____ _____

_____ _____

Name _____ Telephone _____

Address _____ _____

_____ _____

_____ _____

Name

Telephone

Address

---

Name

Telephone

Address

---

Name

Telephone

Address

---

Name

Telephone

Address

---

**A** *friend is one who knows all about you and likes you anyway.*
– CHRISTI MARY WARNER

*T*

*T*

| Name | Telephone |
|------|-----------|
| Address | |

| Name | Telephone |
|------|-----------|
| Address | |

| Name | Telephone |
|------|-----------|
| Address | |

| Name | Telephone |
|------|-----------|
| Address | |

T

Name _____    Telephone _____

Address _____    _____

_____    _____

_____    _____


Name _____    Telephone _____

Address _____    _____

_____    _____

_____    _____


Name _____    Telephone _____

Address _____    _____

_____    _____

_____    _____


Name _____    Telephone _____

Address _____    _____

_____    _____

_____    _____


Do not save your loving speeches
For your friends till they are dead;
Do not write them on their tombstones,
Speak them rather now instead.

– ANNA CUMMINS

*T*

Name _____        Telephone _____

Address _____

_____

_____

_____


Name _____        Telephone _____

Address _____

_____

_____

_____


Name _____        Telephone _____

Address _____

_____

_____

_____


Name _____        Telephone _____

Address _____

_____

_____

_____

*In making dinner for a friend, don't forget the love.*
— JEANNE MOREAU

Name _____  Telephone _____

Address _____  _____

_____  _____

_____  _____

Name _____  Telephone _____

Address _____  _____

_____  _____

_____  _____

Name _____  Telephone _____

Address _____  _____

_____  _____

_____  _____

Name _____  Telephone _____

Address _____  _____

_____  _____

_____  _____

Name _____  Telephone _____

Address _____  _____

_____  _____

_____  _____

*T*

*Name* _____     *Telephone* _____

*Address* _____      _____

_____      _____

_____      _____

*Name* _____     *Telephone* _____

*Address* _____      _____

_____      _____

_____      _____

*Name* _____     *Telephone* _____

*Address* _____      _____

_____      _____

_____      _____

*Name* _____     *Telephone* _____

*Address* _____      _____

_____      _____

_____      _____

*Name* _____     *Telephone* _____

*Address* _____      _____

_____      _____

. . . *The companions of our childhood possess a certain power over our minds which hardly any later friend can obtain.*

– MARY SHELLEY

*T*

Name _____    Telephone _____

Address _____    _____

_____    _____

_____    _____

Name _____    Telephone _____

Address _____    _____

_____    _____

_____    _____

Name _____    Telephone _____

Address _____    _____

_____    _____

_____    _____

Name _____    Telephone _____

Address _____    _____

_____    _____

_____    _____

Name _____    Telephone _____

Address _____    _____

_____    _____

_____    _____

Name _____     Telephone _____

Address _____     _____

_____     _____

_____     _____


Name _____     Telephone _____

Address _____     _____

_____     _____

_____     _____


Name _____     Telephone _____

Address _____     _____

_____     _____

_____     _____


If I knew you and you knew me,
If both of us could clearly see,
And with an inner sight divine,
The meaning of your heart and mine,
I'm sure that we would differ less,
And clasp our hands in friendliness;
Our thoughts would pleasantly agree
If I knew you and you knew me.

– NIXON WATERMAN

$U^V$

# $\mathcal{U}^{\mathcal{V}}$

| | |
|---|---|
| *Name* | *Telephone* |
| *Address* | |
| | |
| | |
| | |
| *Name* | *Telephone* |
| *Address* | |
| | |
| | |
| | |
| *Name* | *Telephone* |
| *Address* | |
| | |
| | |
| *Name* | *Telephone* |
| *Address* | |
| | |
| | |

Name _____     Telephone _____

Address _____

_____

_____

Name _____     Telephone _____

Address _____

_____

_____

Name _____     Telephone _____

Address _____

_____

_____

Name _____     Telephone _____

Address _____

_____

_____

Kind words can be short and easy to speak,
but their echoes are truly endless.

— MOTHER TERESA

Name _____     Telephone _____

Address _____     _____

_____     _____

_____     _____

_____     _____

Name _____     Telephone _____

Address _____     _____

_____     _____

_____     _____

Name _____     Telephone _____

Address _____     _____

_____     _____

_____     _____

Name _____     Telephone _____

Address _____     _____

_____     _____

_____     _____

Name _____     Telephone _____

Address _____     _____

_____     _____

_____     _____

*You* may search my time-worn face,
*You'll* find a merry eye that twinkles
I am NOT an old lady
Just a little girl with wrinkles!

– EDYTHE E. BREGNARD

W

W

| Name | Telephone |
| --- | --- |
| Address | |
| | |
| | |

| Name | Telephone |
| --- | --- |
| Address | |
| | |
| | |

| Name | Telephone |
| --- | --- |
| Address | |
| | |
| | |

| Name | Telephone |
| --- | --- |
| Address | |
| | |
| | |

Name

Telephone

Address

___

Name

Telephone

Address

___

Name

Telephone

Address

___

Name

Telephone

Address

Trouble is part of your life, and if you don't share it, you don't
give the person who loves you a chance to love you enough.

— DINAH SHORE

# W

Name _____  Telephone _____

Address _____  _____

_____  _____

_____  _____


Name _____  Telephone _____

Address _____  _____

_____  _____

_____  _____


Name _____  Telephone _____

Address _____  _____

_____  _____

_____  _____


Name _____  Telephone _____

Address _____  _____

_____  _____

_____  _____


Name _____  Telephone _____

Address _____  _____

_____  _____

_____  _____

*T*here was a definite process by which one made people into friends, and it involved talking to them and listening to them for hours at a time.
                                                                — REBECCA WEST

*W*

Name _____  Telephone _____

Address _____  _____

_____  _____

_____  _____

Name _____  Telephone _____

Address _____  _____

_____  _____

_____  _____

Name _____  Telephone _____

Address _____  _____

_____  _____

_____  _____

Name _____  Telephone _____

Address _____  _____

_____  _____

_____  _____

T*reasure each other in the recognition that we do not know how long we shall have each other.*

–JOSHUA LOTH LIEBMAN

*W*

*Name* _____  *Telephone* _____

*Address* _____ _____

_____ _____

_____ _____

*Name* _____  *Telephone* _____

*Address* _____ _____

_____ _____

_____ _____

*Name* _____  *Telephone* _____

*Address* _____ _____

_____ _____

_____ _____

*Name* _____  *Telephone* _____

*Address* _____ _____

_____ _____

_____ _____

*Name* _____  *Telephone* _____

*Address* _____ _____

_____ _____

_____ _____

# X Y Z

Name _____      Telephone _____

Address _____

_____

_____


Name _____      Telephone _____

Address _____

_____

_____


Name _____      Telephone _____

Address _____

_____

_____


Name _____      Telephone _____

Address _____

_____

_____

Name _____     Telephone _____

Address _____          _____

_____          _____

_____          _____


Name _____     Telephone _____

Address _____          _____

_____          _____

_____          _____


Name _____     Telephone _____

Address _____          _____

_____          _____

_____          _____


Name _____     Telephone _____

Address _____          _____

_____          _____

_____          _____


*The best and most beautiful things in the world cannot be seen or even touched. They must be felt with the heart.*

—HELEN KELLER

$xy^z$

Name _____

Telephone _____

Address _____

_____

_____

_____

Name _____

Telephone _____

Address _____

_____

_____

_____

Name _____

Telephone _____

Address _____

_____

_____

_____

Name _____     Telephone _____

Address _____     _____

_____     _____

_____     _____

Name _____     Telephone _____

Address _____     _____

_____     _____

_____     _____

Name _____     Telephone _____

Address _____     _____

_____     _____

_____     _____

Name _____     Telephone _____

Address _____     _____

_____     _____

_____     _____

_____

O*ne of the signs of passing youth is the birth of a sense of fellowship
with other human beings as we take our place among them.*

– VIRGINIA WOOLF

Name _____  Telephone _____

Address _____  _____

_____  _____

_____  _____

Name _____  Telephone _____

Address _____  _____

_____  _____

_____  _____

Name _____  Telephone _____

Address _____  _____

_____  _____

_____  _____

Name _____  Telephone _____

Address _____  _____

_____  _____

_____  _____

Name _____  Telephone _____

Address _____  _____

_____  _____

_____  _____

Name _____    Telephone _____

Address _____    _____

_____    _____

_____    _____


Name _____    Telephone _____

Address _____    _____

_____    _____

_____    _____


Name _____    Telephone _____

Address _____    _____

_____    _____

_____    _____


Name _____    Telephone _____

Address _____    _____

_____    _____

_____    _____


*But every road is rough to me that has no friend to cheer it.*

– ELIZABETH SHANE

# Notes

*If I don't have friends, then I ain't got nothin'.*

– BILLIE HOLIDAY

# Notes

_____
_____
_____
_____
_____
_____
_____
_____
_____
_____
_____
_____
_____
_____
_____
_____
_____
_____
_____
_____

# Notes

There isn't much that I can do,
But I can sit an hour with you,
And I can share a joke with you,
And sometime share reverses, too . . .
As on our way we go.

— MAUDE PRESTON

# Notes

_____
_____
_____
_____
_____
_____
_____
_____
_____
_____
_____
_____
_____
_____

*The only thing to do is to hug one's friends tight and do one's job.*

— EDITH WHARTON

# Notes

# Notes